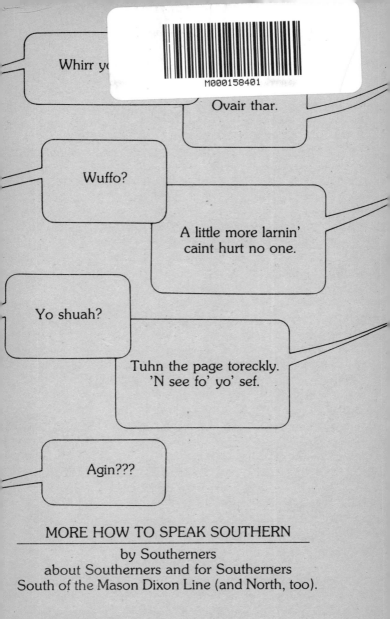

Whirr y...

Ovair thar.

Wuffo?

A little more larnin' caint hurt no one.

Yo shuah?

Tuhn the page toreckly. 'N see fo' yo' sef.

Agin???

MORE HOW TO SPEAK SOUTHERN

by Southerners
about Southerners and for Southerners
South of the Mason Dixon Line (and North, too).

MORE
HOW TO SPEAK
SOUTHERN

by Steve Mitchell
with illustrations by
Sam C. Rawls

BANTAM BOOKS
NEW YORK · TORONTO · LONDON · SYDNEY · AUCKLAND

MORE HOW TO SPEAK SOUTHERN

A Bantam Book / November 1980
9 printings through January 1988

ISBN 0-553-27392-2

Published simultaneously in the United States and Canada

Bantam Books are published by Bantam Books, a division of Bantam Doubleday
Dell Publishing Group, Inc. Its trademark, consisting of the words "Bantam
Books" and the portrayal of a rooster, is Registered in U.S. Patent and
Trademark Office and in other countries. Marca Registrada. Bantam Books,
666 Fifth Avenue, New York, New York 10103.

PRINTED IN THE UNITED STATES OF AMERICA

KR   18   17   16   15   14   13   12   11   10

A

ACit: That's it. "Ah (I) don't wanna hear no more about it. ACit as far as Ah'm concerned."

Addled: Confused, disoriented, as in the case of Northern sociologists who try to make sense out of the South. "What's wrong with that Yankee? He acts right addled."

AD-dress: Where you live. "What's your AD-dress, honey?"

A-DRESS: What women look very good in. "Jeans are nice, but I'd rather see a woman in a-DRESS."

Afar: In a state of combustion. "Call the far department. That house is afar."

Ahce: Solidified liquid that is best employed in the cooling of mint juleps and aged bourbon. "This dry ink (drink) needs more ahce in it."

Ahdin: I didn't. "Ahdin know the gun was loaded, Judge."

Ahr: What we breathe, also a unit of time made up of 60 minutes. "They should've been here about an ahr ago."

Ahreen: A lady's name. "You remember that song that was popular during the Korean War? 'Goodnight, Ahreen?'"

All Ah wanna do is hold you a little, is all: One of the most brazen, outrageous lies Southern men tell women, and always with the utmost sincerity. "All Ah wanna do is hold you a little, is all, honey."

All over hell and half of Georgia: Covering a large area. "Ah've looked for that boy all over hell and half of Georgia."

Ah 'magine: The first word means yourself—or as Southerners say, "yosef," and the second is an expression of intent or belief. "Ah 'magine she's bout the sweetest gull (girl) in Jeff Davis County."

Ails: Else. "Warn't nothin', ma'am. Anybody ails would have done the same thing."

Alms: What beggars ask for in AY-rab countries, but what Southern men hold their girls with. "Ah just want to put my alms around you a little, is all."

AMbolance: A four-wheeled vehicle used to convey the injured to a hospital. "That boy's hurt bad. Better call an ambolance."

Ar: Possessive pronoun. "That's AR dawg, not yours."

Arkensaw: A Southern state some Yankees have been known to confuse with Kansas, even though the two have nothing whatever to do with each other. "She's from Little Rock, Arkensaw."

AH SHOT AN ARRER INTO THE AHR... OWWW....

Arrer: A pointed stick the Indians used to employ with great efficiency, as General George Custer discovered at Little Big Horn. "Ah shot an arrer into the air . . ."

Arthuritis: A painful illness characterized by stiffening of the joints and paralysis. "Grandma's arthuritis is botherin' her real bad today."

Ary: Not any. "He hadn't got ary cent."

At: That. "Is at your car?"

Awficer: A policeman. "Well, Awficer, Ah guess I might have been goin' a little over the speed limit, but, . . ."

Awfullest: The worst. "That's the awfullest lie you ever told me in your life."

B

Babdist: A religious denomination whose members are found in great profusion throughout the South. They are against drinkin' and dancin', but . . . "Ah hear the Babdist preacher run off with the choir director."

Bad-mouth: To disparage or derogate. "All these candidates have bad-mouthed each other so much I've about decided not to vote for any of 'em."

Baws: Your employer. "The baws may not always be right, but he's always the baws."

Bawstun: The largest city in Massachusetts. "King George III didn't like the Bawstun Tea Party much."

Best: Another baffling Southernism that is usually couched in the negative. "You best not speak to Cecil about his car. He just had to spend $300 on it."

DANGED BOBWAR!

Bobwar: A spiky strand of metal used to keep cattle inside an enclosed space. "Watch out, you'll get caught on that bobwar."

Bounden determined: Totally committed to a course of action, not always the wisest. "She's bounden determined to marry him."

Bout: About, except in Tidewater Virginia where it is pronounced "aboot." "It's bout time to put out the fire and call in the dawgs."

Bowut: In Charleston, S.C., a small craft that conveys one across water. "Where's the motor for this bowut?"

THET BOY AINT REAL BRAHT....

Boy: Any Southern white male under the age of 50, usually preceded by the words "good ole," meaning he is amiable, likes a drink now and then and is fond of fishin', huntin' and good-lookin' women. "Clarence is a good ole boy."

Braht: Dazzling. "Venus is a braht planet."

Branch: Part of a tree, but also a small stream. "We'll cross that branch when we come to it."

Bud: Small feathered creature that flies. "A robin sure is a pretty bud."

Cawse: Cause, usually preceded in the South by the adjective "lawst" (lost). "The War Between the States was a lawst cawse."

Cayut: A furry animal much beloved by little girls but detested by adults when it engages in mating rituals in the middle of the night. "Be sure to put the cayut outside before you go to bed."

Chalstun: A city in South Carolina that Yankees call the Cradle of Secession. "Ah don't know why they're so upset. All we wanted was Fort Sumter back."

Chekatawlfarya?: An expression that is rapidly disappearing because of the gasoline shortage, but one that still may be heard by baffled Yankees at service stations in small Southern towns. It translates "Check that oil for you?"

Chitlins: It is said that there are two things you should never see being made: laws and sausages. Chitlins are

another. Chitlins, which can smell up the whole county when being cooked, are boiled and fried hog intestines. Delicious, if you can forget what they are. "Ah'll have another plate of them chitlins."

Chunk: To throw. "Chunk it in there, Leroy. Ole Leroy sure can chunk 'at ball, can't he? Best pitcher we ever had."

Claws: An appendage to a legal document. "You'd be advised to study that claws very carefully."

Clawth: A woven material from which

COLLIE FLARE EAR

cloes (clothes) are made. "Let me have three yards of that clawth, please."

Clone: A type of scent women put on themselves. "What's that clone you got on, honey?"

Collards: A variety of kale, also known as greens. Southerners love them cooked with fatback, also known as the bacon that didn't quite make it. "Pass the collards, please."

Collie flare: A crisp white vegetable that is surprisingly good once you get past the appearance. "Lots of boxers have collie flare ears."

Commence to: To start or engage in

some activity. "They got in a argyment, and the next thing you know, they commence to fight."

Contrack: A legal document, usually heavily in favor of the party who draws it up. "It's just a standard contrack . . . just sign right here."

Contrary: Obstinate, perverse. "Cecil's a fine boy, but she won't have nothin' to do with him. She's just contrary, is all Ah can figure."

Cooter: A large turtle found in Southern streams that supplemented many Dixie diets when the Yankees came down during Reconstruction and carried off everything that wasn't bolted down. "Goin' to the hardware store? Get me some cooter hooks."

Cotta: Our president, at least until the next election. "Did you hear President Cotta on TV last night?"

Crawss: The symbol of Christianity. "Ah love to hear 'em sing 'The Ole Rugged Crawss'."

D

Daints: A more or less formal event in which members of the opposite sex hold each other and move rhythmically to the sound of music. "You wanna go to the daints with me Saturday night, Wilma Sue?"

Damyankee: Anyone who is not from one of the eleven Confederate states. "Ah was ten years old before Ah found out damyankee was two words."

Danjuh: Imminent peril. What John Paul Jones meant when he said "Give me a fast ship, for I intend to put her in harm's way."

Deah: A term of endearment, except in the sense Rhett Butler used it when he said to Scarlett O'Hara, "Frankly, my deah, Ah don't give a damn."

Deppity: A county law enforcement officer. "Bob's a deppity shurf."

Dewk: A prestigious university in North Carolina with an excellent basketball team. "Dewk could go all the way this year."

Dewty: Something that must be done even when it is difficult. "Robert E. Lee said dewty was the most sublime word in the English language."

HONEY... AH THINK IT'S ABOUT TIME YOU WENT ON A DITE...

Didn't go to: Did not intend to. "Don't whip Billy for knockin' his little sister down. He didn't go to do it."

Dite: What people do to lose weight. "Honey, Ah think it's about time you went on a dite."

Dollin: Another term of endearment. President Jimmy Carter got in trouble for calling a woman reporter this. The lady did not realize that Southern men call almost ALL women darling, even those they have met only a few minutes before. "You call EVERYBODY dollin."

Don't differ: Makes no difference. "It don't differ to me whether we go or not."

Down in: Afflicted with spinal pain. "Ole Jim's down in his back."

Draff: A current of chilling air or Selective Service, which is much the same thing in the minds of many young people today. "Ah got a solution to the problem of teenage unrest. Bring back the draff."

Dreckly: Soon. "He'll be along dreckly."

Drinkin' liquor: Exceptionally smooth whiskey. "Ah don't want no fightin' liquor. Gimme a bottle of your best drinkin' liquor."

Duck: Conduit or pipe. "Hand me that roll of duck tape."

Duddinit: Doesn't it. "Duddinit it feel sort of cool in here?"

Dun: To send a bill for money owed. "That finance company's about to dun me to death."

E

Effuts: Exertions. "Lee made great effuts to defeat Grant, but that's hard to do when you're outnumbered three to one."

Everthang: All-encompassing. "Everthang's all messed up."

Everhoo: Another baffling Southernism—a reverse contraction of whoever. "Everhoo one of you kids wants to go to the movie better clean up their room."

F

Fa: A long distance. "Don't git too fa from the house."

Fahn: Excellent. "That sure is a fahn-lookin' woman."

Fair off: A Southern weather report,

FARN LIQUOR

usually delivered by a laconic mountaineer who claims Indian blood and expertise in such matters. "It's stopped rainin'. Looks like it's gonna fair off."

Farn: Anything that is not domestic. "Ah don't drink no farn liquor, specially Rooshin vodka."

Fatnen hawg: Descriptive term applied to the obese. "Put on weight? He's like a fatnen hawg."

Fawl: What happens when you lose your balance. "He tripped over the cayut and took a bad fawl."

Fawn: The instrument a drunken ex-Army buddy uses to call you long distance in the middle of the night to reminisce about old times. "Honey, would you get up and answer the fawn? If it's Billy Bob from Texas, tell him we got divorced and Ah moved up to Alaska."

Fawt: What Yankees and Southerners did when the South asked for a divorce back in 1861 and the North refused to grant it. "Nobody fawt like Stonewall Jackson."

Fawud: Straight ahead, which is the direction General Lee preferred to take. "Fawud, ho!"

ME AND JUNIOR... FLAT OUT!!

Fell off: To have lost weight. "She's not near as fat as she used to be. That girl's fell off a lot."

Fetchin': Attractive. "That's a mighty fetchin' woman. Think Ah'll ask her to daints."

Fizu: Abbreviated version of If I were you. "Fizu, I'd get outta here."

Fladuh: The Sunshine State. "Two things we like to pick in Fladuh are oranges and tourists."

Flat out: A Southern stock car racing expression, meaning put the pedal on the metal and see how fast she'll go.

"Junior Johnson didn't know but one way to drive—flat out."

Fline: To travel by air. "Ah like fline, but why do they make the seats so little and jam 'em so close together?"

Foller: Spies and private detectives spend a lot of time doing this. "Quick . . . Get a cab! We got to foller that car!"

Foolin' around: Can mean not doing anything in particular or sex, usually of the extramarital variety. "Suellen caught her husband foolin' around, so she divorced him."

Fore: Golfers holler it before they hit the little white ball, but it also means prior to in the South. "This was a nice party fore they got here."

Frawg: A greenish amphibian whose legs are much esteemed by diners. "Ah'll have an order of frawg legs, Miss."

Fummeer: A place other than one's present location. "Where do we go fummeer?"

G

Garntee: Any sort of warranty, frequently honored more in the breach than in the observance. "The store said the garntee didn't cover that."

Gawn: Departed. "Debby Lee's not here. She's gawn out with somebody else."

Git own: To expedite matters. "Let's git own with it."

Gone: Going to. "You boys just git out there and play football. We gone make mistakes, but they are, too."

Got a good notion: A statement of intent. "Ah got a good notion to cut a switch and whale the dickens out of that boy."

Got in the wind of: To discover. "Purvis was foolin' around with some topless dancer 'til his wife got in the wind of it and went up side his head with a fryin' pan."

Grain of sense: An appraisal of in-

GRAMMAW GRAMPAW

telligence, invariably expressed in negative terms. "That boy ain't got a grain
of sense."

Grammaw: The Southern matriarch,
both black and white, who is the abso-
lute dictator of most Southern families:
the grandmother. "You better run
home. Grammaw's callin'."

Grampaw: Her male counterpart.
"Grampaw's the head of the house
'cause Grammaw lets him think he
is."

Gummut: A large institution operat-
ing out of Washington that consumes
taxes at a fearful rate. "Bill's got it
made. He's got a gummut job."

H

Hah: High. "Yeah, you can climb that tree, son. Just don't get up too hah."

Hahr: That which grows on your head and requires cutting periodically. "You need a hahrcut."

Haired: A man's first name. "Ah'd like Monday Night Football a lot better without Haired Cosell."

Hawnky-tawnk: A Southern bar or tavern, also known as a jook joint. "Don't you stay out all night at some hawnky-tawnk."

Hod: Not soft, but meaning stubborn

BROKEN HOT

or willful when used to describe a Southern child's head. "That boy's so hod-headed it's pitiful."

Honey: A universal term of address when speaking to female children in the South. "Honey, come here and give grammaw a big kiss."

Hot: A muscle that pumps blood through the body, but also regarded as the center of emotion. "That gull (girl) has just about broke his hot."

Husbun: The male half of a madge (marriage). "He's her second husbun."

Hush yo' mouth: An expression of pleased embarrassment, as when a Southern female is paid an extravagant compliment. "Honey, you're 'bout the sweetest, best-lookin' woman in Tennessee." "Now hush yo' mouth, Bobby Lee Jackson."

If you can't listen, you can feel: What errant Southern children are told just prior to a World Class whipping. "Ah told you to leave that cat alone. If you can't listen, you can feel!"

Ignert: Ignorant. "Ah've figgered out what's wrong with Congress. Most of 'em are just plain ignert."

Ill: Angry, testy. "What's wrong with Mavis today? She's ill as a hornet."

IN-shurnce: A system in which you stand to come into a great deal of money when you die. "Ah'm with the Octopus IN-shurnce Compny. Would it be convenient for me to stop by and talk with you this evenin'?"

Innerduce: To make one person acquainted with another. "Lemme innerduce you to my cousin. She's a little on the heavy side, but she's got a great personality."

Iont: I don't. "Iont know if I can eat another bobbycue (barbecue) or not."

Izril: A nation of which Southerners are inordinately fond, mainly because they respect its fighting ability. "You 'member what Izril done to the AY-rabs in the Six Day War?"

J

Jack-leg: Self-taught, especially in reference to automobile mechanics and clergymen. "He's just a jack-leg preacher, but he sure knows how to put out the hellfire and brimstone."

Jewant: Do you want. "Jewant to go over to the Red Rooster and have a few beers?"

Jookin: To visit a variety of Southern nightspots, many of which are frequented by gentlemen who are armed and dangerous. Jookin mainly involves drinkin', dancin' and, sometimes, fightin'. "Why don't we go jookin tonight, honey?"

K

Ka-yun: A sealed cylinder containing food. "If that woman didn't have a kay-un opener, her family would starve to death."

Kep: Kept. "Ah kep tellin' you not to do that."

Kerosene cat in hell with gasoline drawers on: A colorful Southern expression used as an evaluation of someone's ability to accomplish something. "He ain't got no more chance than a kerosene cat in hell with gasoline drawers on."

Kin: Related to. An Elizabethan expression, one of many which survive in the South. "Are you kin to him?" "Yeah. He's my brother."

LAHTNIN BUG

Klect: To receive money to which one is entitled. "Ah don't think you'll ever klect that bill."

L

Laht: A source of illumination, as in the immortal Hank Williams rendition of "Ah Saw the Laht." "This room's too doc (dark). We need more laht in here."

Lahtnin' bug: A firefly. "You don't see many lahtnin' bugs anymore. Wonder why?"

Lam: Sheep, which most Southerners regard with the deepest possible suspicion as a source of food. "Ah ain't eatin' NOTHIN' that smells like Wildroot Cream Oil, and that's what lam smells like to me."

Lanyop: Lagniappe. In Louisiana, a little something extra. "Ah bought a dozen doughnuts, and he threw in another one as lanyop."

Lar: One who tells untruths. "Not all fishermen are lars. It's just that a lot of lars fish."

Lawg: Part of a tree trunk. "It's phrasin (freezin') in here. Put another lawg on the far."

Layin' up: Resting or meditating. Or as Southern women usually put it, loafing. "Cecil didn't go to work today 'cause of a chronic case of laziness. He's been layin' up in the house all day, drivin' me crazy."

Learn: Teach. "Ah'm gonna take a two-by-four to that mule and learn him some sense."

Lectricty: A mysterious force that gives us heat, illumination, television and all sorts of wondrous things while bringing great profit to the pare (power) companies. "You can't see lectricty, but it's there."

... AND WIF YO HEP... I KIN WIN THIS LEKSHUN.

Lekshun: A political contest. "Who you think's gonna win the lekshun?"

Let alone: Much less. "He can't even hold a job and support himself, let alone support a family."

Let out: Dismissed. "What time does school let out?"

Lick and a promise: To do something in a hurried or perfunctory fashion. "We don't have time to clean this house so it's spotless. Just give it a lick and a promise."

LIE-berry: A building containing thousands upon thousands of literary works.

YOU CALL THIS A LOWANCE...?

"This book's overdue at the LIE-berry."

Lil: Small. "That lil ole puppy sure is cute, ain't he?"

Lowance: A weekly sum of money paid to children in the hope of inducing reasonably good behavior. "Unless you clean up your room, you won't git your lowance this week."

M

Mahty raht: Correct. "You mahty raht about that, Awficer. Guess Ah WAS speedin' a little bit."

Make out: Yes, it means that in the South, too, but it also means finish your meal. "You chirren (children) hadn't had nearly enough to eat. Make out your supper."

Mam: Ma'am, a contraction of madam. A term of respect all Southern younguns (young ones) once were taught to employ when addressing their female elders. "Thank you, mam."

Mawk: Mock; to make fun of, usually by imitating accents or mannerisms. "You ought to hear him mawk President Cotta."

Maul: A shopping center. "You been out to the new maul?"

Mind to: To have the intention of doing something. "Ah got a mind to quit my job and just loaf for a while."

Moon pah: A round, chocolate-covered cake with a marshmallow filling that is traditionally consumed with a Royal Crown Cola, which Southerners refer to as an ArCee. "Let's have a ArCee and a moon pah."

MOON PAH

ARCEE

Motuhsickle: A two-wheeled missile with a powerful engine that is capable of great speed and is inherently unstable, thus providing physicians, hospitals and funeral directors with a regular source of income. "Johnny had his motuhsickle up to 120 last night."

N

Nachur: Nature, but in the sense of sex drive or libido. "When you have a tom cat neutered, it takes away his nachur."

Naht: The opposite of day. "You might say Dracula was a naht person."

Nawth: Any part of the country outside the South—Midwest, California or whatever. If it's not South, it's Nawth. "People from up Nawth sure do talk funny."

Nekkid: To be unclothed. "Did you see her in that new movie? She was nekkid as a jaybird."

Nemmine: Never mind, but used in the sense of difference. "It don't make no nemmine to me."

Nooclar: Having to do with atomic power. "Jake's got a good job over at the nooclar plant."

O

Of a moanin: Of a morning, meaning in the morning. "My daddy always liked his coffee of a moanin."

PART MAKING AIR

Ownliest: The only one. "That's the ownliest one Ah've got left."

P

Pal: Powell. "Ambrose Pal Hill was a good general."

Pannyhos: A misbegotten hybrid of stocking and girdle foisted off on Southern (and American) womanhood by malevolent clothing designers bent on wiping out heterosexuality. "Ah hate pannyhos."

Parts: Buccaneers who sailed under the dreaded skull and crossbones. "See that third baseman? He just signed a big contrack with the Pittsburgh Parts."

Passel: A large quantity. "Ah'm cookin' up a passel of collard greens for supper."

Pattun: A diagram women follow when making clothing. "Ah've got the nicest pattun for a new Easter dress."

Pawl: A man's name. "Pawl was one of the 12 disciples."

PEEcans: Northerners call them pe-CONNS for some obscure reason, but they are thin-shelled nuts that translate themselves wonderfully into the Southern delicacy called PEEcan pie. "Honey, go out in the yard and pick up a passel of PEEcans. Ah'm gonna make us a pie."

Pert: Perky, full of energy. "You look mighty pert today."

Picked up: To have gained weight. "You've picked up a little."

Pick at: To pester and annoy. "Jimmy,

Ah told you not to pick at your little sister. If you can't listen, you can feel."

Pinny: The 100th part of a dollar and so valueless these days that most people don't even pick them up when they drop them. "Ah don't owe him a pinny."

Pleece: Law enforcement officers. "Is that a pleece car behind us?"

Pup: What they turn trees into to make paper. "Ah'm gonna beat him to a pup."

Purtiest: The most pretty. "Ain't she the purtiest thing you ever seen?"

Q

Quar: An organized choral group, usually connected with a church or school. "Did you hear the news? The preacher left his wife and run off with the quar director."

R

Raffle: A long-barreled firearm. "Dan'l

WHOOEEE...THAT'S SOME RAFFLE!

Boone was a good shot with a raffle."

Rahtnaow: At once. "Linda Sue, Ah want you to tell that boy it's time to go home and come in the house rahtnaow."

Rahts: Rights. "When I asked those Johnny Reb prisoners what they were fighting for, I thought they said they were fighting for their rats."

Ranch: A tool used to loosen or tighten nuts and bolts. "Hand me that ranch, Homer."

Rare back: What a horse does just prior to throwing you off the saddle. "When you see a cobra rare back, you know he's gettin' ready to strike."

Raut: A method of getting from one place to another which Southerners pronounce to rhyme with "kraut." Yankees, for reasons that remain shrouded in mystery, pronounce "route" to rhyme with "root." Or worse still, "foot."

Rawsin: The sap that oozes from pine trees. "Fiddlers put rawsin on their bows."

Redbugs: Chiggers. "Put some insek (insect) spray on your legs so you don't get redbugs."

Reckonize: The realization of seeing something familiar. "Why, you're the fella that plays the Lone Ranger on TV. Ah didn't reckonize you without your mast (mask)."

Recud: Round pieces of plastic that emit music when played on a stereo. "That's a nice recud. Play it again."

Rester: To be accounted for by the guvmint. "You kids today are lucky. When Ah was your age, Ah had to

WUK? NAW...
RETARD.

rester for the draff. They almost got
me, too."

Restrunt: A place to eat. "New York's
got a lot of good restrunts."

Retard: No longer employed. "He's
retard now."

Ruut: The underground part of a tree
which Southerners rightly pronounce
to rhyme with "toot." Yankees pronounce it to rhyme with "foot." Nobody knows why.

S

Sass: Another Elizabethan term derived from the word saucy, meaning to speak in an impertinent manner. "Don't sass me, young lady. You're not too old to get a whippin'."

Sayul: Sale. Some radio announcers, in a misguided attempt to sound sophisticated, pronounce it to rhyme with "sell;" "Don't miss the big sell."

Scapped: An unpleasant operation formerly carried out by Indians. "That barber scapped you."

Scuse: To beg someone's pardon. "Scuse me, ma'am."

Sebmlebm: A convience store. "Stop by the Sebmlebm and get me a six-pack of beer."

Sebmty: A ripe old age—seven decades, to be exact. "He's sebmty years old."

WHO STEPPED IN MY SEEMENT?

SEE-ment: A mixture that turns into concrete. "Be careful and don't step on that wet SEE-ment."

SEM-eye: Partially. "Did you see that movie 'SEM-eye Tough?'"

Set: Sit. "Come on in and set a spell."

Shainteer: Indicates the absence of a female. "Is the lady of the house in?" "Nope. Shainteer."

Share: To cleanse oneself with water. "Why does somebody always call up when Ah'm takin' a share?"

Shudenoughta; Should not. "You shudenoughta have another drink."

Shuhmun: The Yankee general, William Tecumseh, who said "War is hell" and proved it. "Shuhmun burned Etlanna (Atlanta)."

Skawld: To burn with hot water. "You have to skawld a hawg after you kill it."

Slip off: To absent oneself, usually by stealth. "Where'd that boy slip off to? He was right here a minute ago."

Spaded: To render a female animal incapable of producing offspring. "You ought to have that cat spaded before she has anymore kittens."

Speakuh: One who speaks. "Who's the Speakuh of the House?"

Spearmint: Something scientists do. "Dr. Frankenstein decided to do this spearmint, see, and he ended up with a monster."

Spell: An indeterminate length of time. "Let's sit here and rest a spell."

Spose: Suppose. "Spose you and me was to get married?"

Srimp: A small crustacean much beloved by residents of the Guff (Gulf) Coast. "They sure love srimp and crawfish in Loosiana."

Stain: The opposite of leaving. "Ah hate this party, and Ah'm not stain much longer."

Steal: What they make moonshine in. "The revenoors found pappy's steal."

Story: The polite euphemism for an untruth. "She said she was stain' home tonight. That girl told me a story!"

Squeezins: What they make in steals— a volatile derivative of corn also known as moonshine, shine and white liquor. "Ah wouldn't mind havin' a little drink of squeezins about now."

Supper: The evening meal Southerners are having while Yankees are having dinner. "What's for supper, honey?"

Swaller: To transfer from the mouth to the stomach. "My throat's so sore Ah can't hardly swaller."

Swayge down: The process of a swollen area returning to normal, derived from the Old English "assuage." "If you lance a boil, it'll swayge down."

T

Tah: A useless appurtenance men feel compelled to wear around their necks. "Ah hate to wear a tah."

Take on: To behave in a highly emotional manner. "Don't take on like that, Brenda Sue. He's not the only man in Lee County."

Taken: Took. "You won't go wrong on that blue Ford. Ah taken it in trade off a Sunday School teacher. Don't use a drop of oil."

Tal: What you dry off with after you take a share. "Would you bring me a tal, sweetheart?"

Tamarr: The day after today. "Tamarr's a school day."

Tapern: To narrow to a point. "W.C. don't drink near as much as he used to. He's tapern off."

Tare: To rip, also a high building. "Over in Italy, we saw the Leanin' Tare of Pizza."

Tawt: To instruct. "Don't pull that cat's tail. Ah tawt you better'n that."

Tewsdee: The day before Wednesday. "If this is Mondee, tamarr must be Tewsdee."

Teyun: The number that comes after nine. "He's broke all the Teyun Commandments but one, and that's just 'cause he couldn't figure out how to make graven images."

Thank: Think. "Ah thank Ah'll go to a movie tonight."

DICK'S HATBAND

DICK

Tharties: Authorities, usually police and prosecutors. "Don't take that money, Congressman. It could be from the tharties."

That ole dawg won't hunt no more: That will not work. "You want to borrow $20 when you still owe me fifty? That ole dawg won't hunt no more."

Thawt: The process of thinking. "He's lawst in thawt."

They: There. "They ain't no use tryin' to fight City Hall."

Thoo: Finished, completed. "Ah'm bout thoo with this book."

Tight as Dick's hatband: Stingy. It is not known who Dick was or why his hatband was so tight or what any of it has to do with being close with a dollar, but folks down South still say "Him loan you money? He's tight as Dick's hatband."

Throw off on: To cast aspersions. "Don't throw off on my new car."

Til the last pea's out of the dish: To remain at a social gathering for an unconscionably long time. "They'll stay til the last pea's out of the dish."

Tore up: Distraught, very upset. "His wife just left him, and he's all tore up about it."

Tother: One or the other. "You can have this one, or you can take tother one."

Troll: State trooper. "Ah got stopped by the highway troll on I-95."

Twict: One more than once. "Ah've told you once. Ah'm not gonna tell you twict."

U

Uhmewzin: Funny, comical. "Few things are more uhmewzin than a Yankee tryin' to affect a Southern accent, since they invariably address one person as 'y'all when any Southern six-year-old knows 'y'all is always plural because it means 'all of you.'"

Unbeknownst: Lacking knowledge of. "Unbeknownst to them, he had marked the cards."

Usta: Used to. "Ah usta live in Savannah."

V

Vaymuch: Not a whole lot, when expressed in the negative. "Ah don't like this ham vaymuch."

W

Wahn: What Jesus turned the water into, unless you're a Babdist who is persuaded it was only grape juice. "Could Ah have another glass of that wahn?"

AHH... FRUIT OF THE VINE... WAHN

Wars: Slender strands of coated copper that carry power over long distances. "They're puttin' telephone wars underground now."

Warsh: To cleanse one's body, often with the aid of a warshrag, known to Yankees as a washcloth. "We need to find a carwarsh someplace."

Waw: A conflict between military forces. "My great-grandpaw fought in the Waw for Southern Independence."

Wawk: A method of non-polluting travel by foot. "Why don't we take an old-fashioned wawk?"

Wawl: A partition used to separate rooms. "The wawls in these new apartment buildings sure are thin. Kind of embarrassin' when the people next door are newlyweds."

Wear out: An expression used to describe a highly-effective method of behavior modification in children. "When Ah get ahold of that boy, Ah'm gonna wear him out."

Wender: A glass-covered opening in a wawl. "Open that wender. It's too hot in here."

What: The absence of color. "Mark Twain liked to wear what suits."

Whirl: Where will. "Whirl you spend eternity?" "With my luck, probably in Newark."

Win: An unseen force that propels sailboats. "We're not gittin' anywhere. The win's died down."

Winsheel: What you see through when you drive a car. "Remember when service station attendants used to clean your winsheel?"

Won't: Was not—an eastern North Carolina expression. "Ah didn't do it. It won't me."

Wooden: Would not. "Ah wooden do that if Ah was you."

Wooden hit a lick at a snake: Lazy, or as Southerners say, sorry. "He's too sorry to hit a lick at a snake."

Y

Yat: A common greeting in the Irish Channel section of New Orleans. Instead of saying "hey" in lieu of "hello" the way most Southerners do, they say "Where yat?"

Yeller: One of the primary colors. "A labor union would call this a yeller dawg contrack."

Yesterdee: The day before today. "Where were you yesterdee?"

Yew: Not a tree, but a personal pronoun. "Yew wanna shoot some pool?"

Y'heah?: A redundant expression tacked onto the end of sentences by

Southerners. "Y'all come back soon, y'heah?"

Yontny: Do you want any. "Yontny more cornbread?"

Yore: Another personal pronoun, this one denoting ownership. "Where's yore wife tonight?"

Yungins: Also spelled younguns, meaning young ones. "Ah want all you yungins in bed in five minutes."

Z

Zit: Is it. "Zit already midnight, sugar? Tahm sure flies when you're havin' fun."

Steve Mitchell,
a North Carolinian, is
a columnist for the
Palm Beach (Fla.) Post.

Sam C. Rawls,
a Florida cracker, is
the chief cartoonist
for the Palm Beach Post.

Both are lazy
and would rather go
bass fishing than work.